THE ART

STRATEGIES OF WAR

THIS IS HOW I FIGHT MY BATTLES

MARK PICKETT

CONTENT

ABOUT THE AUTHOR 3

INTRODUCTION 6

KEY NOTE 8

STRATEGY 1 12

STRATEGY 2 16

STRATEGY 3 20

STRATEGY 4 24

STRATEGY 5 28

STRATEGY 6 32

STRATEGY 7 37

STRATEGY 8 43

STRATEGY 9 48

STRATEGY 10 52

CONCLUSION 56

WARFARE PRAYER 58

ABOUT THE AUTHOR

Mark Pickett is a devoted husband and loving father of two children. While his professional accomplishments and ministry endeavors are notable, Mark's greatest joy and fulfillment come from his role as a husband and father. Mark is a dynamic and influential leader in the Christian community, serving as the Senior Pastor of Influence Church, a thriving congregation with two locations. With a passion for equipping and empowering individuals, Mark has also made a significant impact as an author, life coach, and mentor. Additionally, he holds the esteemed position of Governing Apostle of AMP Global and MAPS Network, further expanding his reach and influence.

As the Senior Pastor of Influence Church, Mark Pickett has a heart for seeing lives transformed and communities impacted by the power of the gospel. With a commitment to biblical teaching, authentic worship, and compassionate outreach, he has led Influence Church to become a vibrant and diverse community of believers. Under his leadership, the church has experienced remarkable growth, both spiritually and numerically, with a focus on empowering individuals to live out their God-given purpose.

Beyond his pastoral role, Mark is an accomplished author, with several books that have inspired and challenged readers to deepen their faith and pursue a life of purpose. His writings reflect his deep understanding of Scripture and his ability to communicate profound spiritual truths in a practical and relatable manner. Through his books, Mark continues to impact lives and encourage individuals to live with intentionality and passion for Christ.

Recognized for his wisdom and insight, Mark Pickett also serves as a life coach and mentor to individuals seeking personal and spiritual growth. With a compassionate and discerning approach, he empowers individuals to discover their unique gifts and talents, overcome obstacles, and live a life of significance. Through one-on-one coaching and mentoring relationships, Mark has helped countless individuals navigate life's challenges and experience breakthroughs in their personal and professional lives.

In addition to his local ministry and coaching endeavors, Mark Pickett holds the esteemed position of Governing Apostle of AMP Global and MAPS Network. In this role, he provides leadership, guidance, and oversight to a network of churches and ministries, both nationally and internationally. His passion for unity, collaboration, and global impact has positioned him as a respected leader within the Christian community. Mark Pickett's life and ministry are marked by a deep love for God, a commitment to excellence, and a heart for seeing individuals reach their full potential in Christ. His dedication to biblical teaching, his passion for mentoring and coaching, and his visionary leadership have made him a trusted and influential figure within the Christian community. Through his various roles and endeavors, Mark continues to inspire and empower individuals to live a life of purpose, influence, and transformation.

INTRODUCTION

We often find ourselves facing battles that extend beyond the physical realm. These battles are not fought with conventional weapons or brute force, but rather with spiritual strategies that are rooted in the timeless wisdom of Scripture. As the apostle Paul aptly stated, *"For though we live in the world, we do not wage war as the world does. The weapons we fight with are not the weapons of the world"* (**2 Corinthians 10:3-4**).

In this book, we will dive into the realm of spiritual warfare, exploring the principles and strategies that enable us to overcome the forces of darkness and walk in victory. Drawing inspiration from the Scriptures, particularly the exhortation of Paul to *"put on the whole armor of God"* (**Ephesians 6:11**), we will uncover powerful truths and practical insights that equip us to fight our battles with confidence and faith.

Each strategy given will unveil a plan of victory over the enemy, guiding you through the spiritual landscape and providing you with the tools necessary to engage in effective spiritual warfare. From the importance of prayer and intercession to the significance of discernment and spiritual authority, we will explore a wide range of strategies that empower us to stand firm against the schemes of the enemy.

Throughout this journey, it is important to remember that we do not fight alone. The battles we face are not ours alone to bear, but rather, we have a faithful and mighty God who fights on our behalf. As we align ourselves with His purposes and rely on His strength, we will discover that victory is not only possible but inevitable.

So, I invite you to embark on this transformative journey of discovering the strategies for spiritual warfare. Together, let us learn how to fight our battles with the wisdom and power that comes from above, declaring with confidence**, "THIS IS HOW I FIGHT MY BATTLES!**

KEY NOTE

WEAPONS ARE NOT CARNAL
"For the weapons of our warfare are not carnal but mighty in God for pulling down strongholds" (**2 Corinthians 10:4**).

In his second letter to the Corinthians, the apostle Paul addresses a variety of issues and challenges faced by the church in Corinth. One particular aspect he emphasizes is the nature of the weapons that believers should employ in their spiritual warfare. Paul makes it clear that the weapons of a Christian are not carnal or worldly, but rather spiritual and powerful.

These words hold great significance for believers, reminding us that our battle is not fought with physical weapons but with the spiritual resources and authority given to us by God. The apostle begins by contrasting the weapons of the world with the weapons of our warfare. Carnal weapons are those that are physical in nature, such as swords, spears, or other instruments of war. While these may be effective in earthly battles, they are inadequate when it comes to the spiritual realm. The battles we face as believers are not against flesh and blood, but against spiritual forces of darkness (Ephesians 6:12). Therefore, our weapons must be suited for this spiritual warfare.

The purpose of these spiritual weapons is to pull down strongholds. Strongholds can be understood as spiritual fortresses or barriers that the enemy establishes in our lives. They can take the form of false beliefs, sinful habits, or any other stronghold that hinders our relationship with God. These strongholds can only be effectively dismantled through the use of spiritual weapons. So, what are these spiritual weapons that Paul is referring to? While he does not provide an exhaustive list in this particular verse, throughout his writings, Paul does mention several key weapons that believers can employ. The weapons are:

- **PRAYER** – Prayer is a powerful weapon that allows us to communicate with God, seek His guidance, and intercede on behalf of others.
- **THE WORD OF GOD** – The Word is a sharp sword that pierces through deception and brings light and truth into our lives.
- **FAITH** – Faith enables us to trust in God's promises and overcome the doubts and fears that the enemy throws our way.
- **THE HOLY SPIRIT**- The Holy Spirit empowers and guides us in our spiritual battles.
- **PRAISE** – Praise is a weapon that shifts our focus from our circumstances to the greatness and faithfulness of God. And the armor of God equips us for the spiritual warfare we face.

By utilizing these spiritual weapons, believers can effectively wage war against the enemy's schemes and pull down the strongholds that hinder our spiritual growth and relationship with God. It is important to remember that our weapons are not carnal but mighty in God. They are not limited by human strength, but rather by the power and authority of the One who equips us for battle.

As we navigate the challenges and spiritual battles of life, let us be mindful of the weapons at our disposal. Let us rely on the power of God, armed with prayer, the Word, faith, the Holy Spirit, praise, and the armor of God. With these spiritual weapons, we can confidently face any stronghold that stands in our way, knowing that victory is assured in Christ.

THE STRATEGIES OF WAR

STRATEGY 1

PRAYING IN THE SPIRIT

Ephesians 6:18 - *"And pray in the Spirit on all occasions with all kinds of prayers and requests. With this in mind, be alert and always keep on praying for all the Lord's people."*

This verse comes from the Apostle Paul's letter to the Ephesians, where he provides instructions on spiritual warfare and the armor of God. In this particular verse, Paul emphasizes the importance of prayer in the life of a believer, especially in the context of spiritual warfare. Paul encourages believers to engage in prayer in the Spirit, which refers to praying under the guidance and influence of the Holy Spirit.

Paul's instruction to pray **"on all occasions"** emphasizes the need for a consistent and ongoing prayer life. Prayer is not meant to be limited to specific times or situations but should be a continual practice in the life of a believer. It is through prayer that we maintain a constant connection with God, seeking His guidance, wisdom, and strength. Paul also emphasizes the importance of praying with **"all kinds of prayers and requests."** This encompasses various forms of prayer, including intercession, supplication, thanksgiving, and praise. Each type of prayer serves a unique purpose and allows believers to express their hearts to God in different ways. Through these diverse forms of prayer, we can bring our needs, concerns, and praises before God.

Furthermore, Paul exhorts believers to be **"alert"** and to "keep on praying for all the Lord's people." This highlights the communal aspect of prayer. We are not only called to pray for ourselves but also to intercede for others. By lifting up the needs of fellow believers, we participate in the spiritual battle together, supporting and encouraging one another. The text emphasizes the importance of prayer in the life of a believer, particularly in the context of spiritual warfare. It encourages believers to pray in the Spirit, with different types of prayers, and to remain vigilant and persistent in prayer. Through prayer, we tap into the power and guidance of God, equipping ourselves for the battles we face and supporting others in their spiritual journey.

TYPES OF PRAYERS IN WARFARE

Prayer is a vital component of our spiritual warfare as believers. It is through prayer that we communicate with God, seek His guidance, and invite His power into our lives and circumstances. One powerful strategy in our prayer life is praying in the Spirit, also known as praying in tongues or praying in the Holy Spirit. This form of prayer allows us to tap into the supernatural resources and wisdom of God. Here is a strategy on how to incorporate praying in the Spirit in our spiritual warfare:

1. **INTERCESSORY PRAYER**

Praying on behalf of others is a powerful way to engage in spiritual warfare. Interceding for others allows us to stand in the gap and plead for God's intervention and protection in their lives.

2. **PRAYERS OF REPENTANCE**

Recognizing our own sins and repenting before God is crucial in spiritual warfare. Confessing our sins and seeking God's forgiveness opens the way for His power and victory to manifest in our lives.

3. **PRAYERS OF DECLARATION**

Speaking God's promises and truths over our lives and situations is a form of warfare. By declaring God's Word, we align ourselves with His truth and invite His power to work in and through us.

4. **PRAYERS OF PRAISE AND THANKSGIVING**

Praising and thanking God in the midst of spiritual battles is a powerful act of warfare. It shifts our focus from the problem to the greatness of God and strengthens our faith in His ability to overcome.

5. **PRAYERS IN THE SPIRIT**

Praying in tongues or praying in the Holy Spirit is a unique form of prayer that allows us to tap into the supernatural resources and wisdom of God. It is a powerful weapon in spiritual warfare, as the Spirit intercedes through us with groanings that cannot be expressed in words (Romans 8:26)

SCRIPTURES TO STUDY

James 5:16: *"Therefore confess your sins to each other and pray for each other so that you may be healed. The prayer of a righteous person is powerful and effective."*

2 Chronicles 7:14: *"If my people, who are called by my name, will humble themselves and pray and seek my face and turn from their wicked ways, then I will hear from heaven, and I will forgive their sin and will heal their land."*

Matthew 26:41: *"Watch and pray so that you will not fall into temptation. The spirit is willing, but the flesh is weak."*

ASK YOURSELF

- How can I cultivate a lifestyle of praying in the Spirit?

_____
_____
_____
_____

- What are some practical ways to incorporate praying in the Spirit into my daily routine?

1. _____
2. _____
3. _____
4. _____

STRATEGY 2

RENEWING YOUR MIND WITH THE WORD OF GOD

Romans 12:2 *"Do not conform to the pattern of this world, but be transformed by the renewing of your mind. Then you will be able to test and approve what God's will is—his good, pleasing and perfect will."*

The apostle Paul addresses the believers in Rome, urging them to live a transformed life in Christ. In Romans 12:2, he specifically talks about the importance of renewing the mind.

Understanding the Mind

The mind is a powerful tool that shapes our thoughts, attitudes, and actions. It is the battleground where our beliefs, desires, and emotions collide. When we accept Jesus Christ as our Savior, our spirits are renewed, but our minds still need transformation. Our old ways of thinking, influenced by the world, sin, and our own flesh, need to be replaced with the truth of God's Word.

The Call to Renewal

Romans 12:2 states, *"Do not conform to the pattern of this world, but be transformed by the renewing of your mind. Then you will be able to test and approve what God's will is—his good, pleasing and perfect will."* This verse highlights the need to break free from the conformity to the world's standards and instead align our minds with God's truth.

Renewing the mind is a vital aspect of the Christian journey. It involves breaking free from the patterns of the world, embracing God's truth, transforming our thoughts and beliefs, and experiencing the result of a renewed mind. As we commit to this process, we will grow in our relationship with God, live out His will, and become more like Christ. Let us continuously renew our minds, allowing God to transform us from the inside out.

Strategies for a Renewed Mind for Spiritual Warfare:

1. **PRAYER AND SEEKING GOD'S GUIDANCE**

    Begin each day with prayer, seeking God's wisdom, strength, and guidance. Ask Him to reveal any areas of your mind that need renewal and to help you overcome the enemy's attacks. Invite the Holy Spirit to lead you in the battle.

2. **IMMERSION IN GOD'S WORD**

    Regularly study and meditate on Scripture to fill your mind with God's truth. Memorize key verses that address the specific areas of struggle or temptation you face. The Word of God is a powerful weapon against the enemy's lies and deception.

3. **GUARDING YOUR THOUGHT LIFE**

    Be vigilant in guarding your thoughts. Take captive every thought that goes against God's truth and replace it with His Word. Avoid entertainment, media, and conversations that promote negative or sinful thinking. Surround yourself with positive and uplifting influences.

4. **POSITIVE AFFIRMATIONS**

   Speak positive affirmations based on God's Word over your mind and life. Declare truths about your identity in Christ and His power at work within you. This helps to counteract negative self-talk and build a strong foundation of faith.

5. **WORSHIP AND PRAISE**

   Engage in regular times of worship and praise, both individually and corporately. Worship shifts our focus from ourselves to God and magnifies His greatness. It helps to renew our minds and reminds us of His power and faithfulness.

6. **RENEWING THE MIND THROUGH FASTING**

   Consider incorporating fasting into your spiritual warfare strategy. Fasting helps to discipline the flesh and heighten spiritual sensitivity. It can be a powerful tool to break strongholds, seek God's guidance, and renew the mind.

7. **SEEKING DELIVERANCE AND INNER HEALING**

   If you are struggling with deep-rooted issues or spiritual strongholds, seek the help of mature and trusted spiritual leaders who can guide you through deliverance and inner healing. Sometimes, renewing the mind requires addressing underlying wounds and traumas.

SCRIPTURES TO STUDY

Philippians 4:8 *"Finally, brothers and sisters, whatever is true, whatever is noble, whatever is right, whatever is pure, whatever is lovely, whatever is admirable—if anything is excellent or praiseworthy—think about such things."*

2 Corinthians 10:5 *"We demolish arguments and every pretension that sets itself up against the knowledge of God, and we take captive every thought to make it obedient to Christ."*

Ephesians 4:23 *"Be renewed in the spirit of your minds."*

Colossians 3:2 *"Set your minds on things above, not on earthly things."*

Isaiah 26:3 *"You will keep in perfect peace those whose minds are steadfast because they trust in you."*

2 Timothy 1:7 *"For God has not given us a spirit of fear, but of power and of love and of a sound mind."*

Romans 8:6 *"The mind governed by the flesh is death, but the mind governed by the Spirit is life and peace."*

As you reflect on these scriptures, meditate on their meaning, and allow them to shape your thoughts and beliefs. Let them guide you in renewing your mind and aligning your thinking with God's truth.

ASK YOURSELF

- What are some effective methods for renewing my mind with God's Word?

1. _____
2. _____

STRATEGY 3

PUTTING ON THE ARMOR OF GOD

Ephesians 6:11 *"Put on the full armor of God, so that you can take your stand against the devil's schemes."*

Paul writes, *"Put on the full armor of God so that you can take your stand against the devil's schemes"* (Ephesians 6:11). These words hold immense significance for believers in every generation, reminding us that we are engaged in a spiritual warfare that requires divine protection and preparation.

1. **BELT OF TRUTH**

    Just as a belt holds everything together, truth is the foundation of our spiritual life. It is through the truth of God's Word that we can discern right from wrong, and it guards us against the lies and deceptions of the enemy. The truth keeps us grounded in God's promises and helps us to walk in righteousness.

2. **BREASTPLATE OF RIGHTEOUSNESS**

    This piece of armor guards our hearts and protects us from the attacks of the enemy. Righteousness is not something we can achieve on our own, but it is imputed to us through faith in Christ. By living in obedience to God's commands and relying on His grace, we can stand firm against the accusations and temptations of the devil.

3. **FOOTWEAR OF THE GOSPEL OF PEACE**

This footwear enables us to stand firm and be ready to share the good news of Jesus Christ with others. It represents our readiness to bring the message of peace and reconciliation to a broken world. As we walk in the truth and live out the gospel, we become instruments of God's peace, bringing hope to those around us.

4. **SHIELD OF FAITH**

This shield is not just any shield but a shield of faith. Faith is our trust and confidence in God's promises and character. It is through faith that we can extinguish the fiery darts of doubt, fear, and temptation that the enemy hurls at us. Faith enables us to stand strong, knowing that God is with us and will never forsake us.

5. **HELMET OF SALVATION**

Just as a helmet protects the head, the helmet of salvation guards our minds. It reminds us of the eternal hope we have in Christ and protects us from the enemy's attacks on our thoughts and beliefs. When we are secure in our salvation, we can confidently face any spiritual battle that comes our way.

6. **SWORD OF THE SPIRIT**

The Word of God is a powerful weapon that we can wield against the enemy's lies and deceptions. It is through the Scriptures that we gain wisdom, find guidance, and receive revelation from God. By meditating on and applying God's

Word in our lives, we can effectively combat the enemy's schemes.

Wearing the Armor of God helps Christians to stay grounded in truth, live with righteousness, spread the message of peace, defend against doubts and attacks, maintain their salvation, and utilize the power of God's Word. It serves as a reminder of the spiritual battle that Christians face and the need to rely on God's strength and protection. May we walk in the power and protection of God's armor, knowing that He has equipped us for every spiritual battle we may face.

SCRIPTURES TO STUDY

Ephesians 6:14-17 *"Stand firm then, with the belt of truth buckled around your waist, with the breastplate of righteousness in place, and with your feet fitted with the readiness that comes from the gospel of peace. In addition to all this, take up the shield of faith, with which you can extinguish all the flaming arrows of the evil one. Take the helmet of salvation and the sword of the Spirit, which is the word of God."*

Romans 13:12 *"The night is nearly over; the day is almost here. So let us put aside the deeds of darkness and put on the armor of light."*

1 Thessalonians 5:8 *"But since we belong to the day, let us be sober, putting on faith and love as a breastplate, and the hope of salvation as a helmet."*

ASK YOURSELF

- How can I practically put on the armor of God in my daily life?

_____

_____

_____

- What are some specific ways to utilize each piece of the armor of God in spiritual warfare?

    1. _____
    2. _____
    3. _____
    4. _____

STRATEGY 4

EXERCISING SPIRITUAL DISCERNMENT

1 John 4:1 *"Dear friends, do not believe every spirit, but test the spirits to see whether they are from God, because many false prophets have gone out into the world."*

Exercising spiritual discernment is an important aspect of a believer's journey. Here are some strategies to help you develop and practice spiritual discernment:

1. **SEEK A PERSONAL RELATIONSHIP WITH GOD**

    Developing a close relationship with God through prayer, meditation, and studying His Word is essential. The more you know God and His character, the better you will be able to discern His will and guidance.

2. **CULTIVATE A TEACHABLE AND HUMBLE SPIRIT**

    Recognize that you don't have all the answers and be open to learning from others who have wisdom and spiritual maturity. Humility allows you to be receptive to the leading of the Holy Spirit and to consider different perspectives.

3. **STUDY AND MEDITATE ON SCRIPTURE**

    Regularly read and study the Bible to gain a deeper understanding of God's truth and principles. Scripture is a reliable guide that can help you discern between what is of God and what is not.

4. **SURROUND YOURSELF WITH WISE AND DISCERNING BELIEVERS**

   Seek out the company of fellow believers who demonstrate spiritual discernment and wisdom. Engage in discussions and seek their counsel when facing important decisions or situations.

5. **PRAY FOR WISDOM AND GUIDANCE**

   Ask God to grant you wisdom and discernment in all areas of your life. Pray for the Holy Spirit to guide you, reveal truth, and help you distinguish between right and wrong.

6. **TEST EVERYTHING AGAINST GOD'S WORD**

   When faced with decisions or situations, compare them to the teachings and principles found in the Bible. God's Word serves as a reliable standard against which all things can be measured.

7. **LISTEN TO THE HOLY SPIRIT**

   Be attentive to the promptings and convictions of the Holy Spirit within you. The Holy Spirit is our guide and counselor, and He can help us discern the truth and make wise choices.

By consistently seeking Him and applying these strategies, you can develop and exercise spiritual discernment in your daily life.

SCRIPTURES TO STUDY

Proverbs 2:6-7 *"For the Lord gives wisdom; from his mouth come knowledge and understanding; he stores up sound wisdom for the upright; he is a shield to those who walk in integrity."*

James 1:5 *"If any of you lacks wisdom, let him ask God, who gives generously to all without reproach, and it will be given him."*

Romans 12:2 *"Do not conform to the pattern of this world, but be transformed by the renewing of your mind. Then you will be able to test and approve what God's will is—his good, pleasing and perfect will."*

1 Corinthians 2:14 *"The person without the Spirit does not accept the things that come from the Spirit of God but considers them foolishness, and cannot understand them because they are discerned only through the Spirit.*

Hebrews 5:14 *"But solid food is for the mature, who by constant use have trained themselves to distinguish good from evil."*

Psalm 119:105 *"Your word is a lamp for my feet, a light on my path."*

1 John 4:1 *"Dear friends, do not believe every spirit, but test the spirits to see whether they are from God because many false prophets have gone out into the world."*

Reflecting on these scriptures can help you gain insights into the importance of seeking wisdom from God, renewing your mind, relying on the guidance of the Holy Spirit, and testing everything against God's Word. Take time to meditate on these verses, pray for understanding, and allow God to speak to your heart as you seek to exercise spiritual discernment in your life.

ASK YOURSELF

- How can I develop my spiritual discernment to distinguish between the voices of God and the enemy?

  _____
  _____
  _____
  _____

- What are some practical steps I can take to test the spirits and discern the truth?

1. _____
   _____
2. _____
3. _____

STRATEGY 5

WALKING IN THE AUTHORITY OF CHRIST

Luke 10:19 *"I have given you authority to trample on snakes and scorpions and to overcome all the power of the enemy; nothing will harm you."*

Walking in the authority of Christ is an empowering and transformative experience. Here is a strategy to help you walk in the authority that Christ has given you:

1. **KNOW YOUR IDENTITY IN CHRIST**

    Understand that as a believer, you are a child of God and have been given authority through Jesus Christ. Recognize that you are a new creation, forgiven, and empowered by the Holy Spirit.

2. **SUBMIT TO GOD'S WILL AND ALIGN WITH HIS PURPOSES**

    Surrender your own desires and ambitions to God's will. Seek to align your thoughts, words, and actions with His purposes, relying on His guidance and direction.

3. **WALK IN OBEDIENCE TO GOD'S COMMANDS**

    Live a life of obedience to God's Word and the teachings of Jesus. Obeying God's commands and living a life of righteousness enables you to walk in the authority that Christ has given you.

4. **EXERCISE FAITH**

   Trust in God's promises and exercise faith in His power and authority. Believe that as a child of God, you have been given the authority to overcome challenges, resist temptation, and walk in victory.

5. **BE FILLED WITH THE HOLY SPIRIT**

   Continually seek to be filled with the Holy Spirit, allowing Him to empower and guide you in walking in the authority of Christ. Yield to His leading and rely on His strength.

6. **USE YOUR AUTHORITY FOR GOD'S GLORY AND THE BENEFIT OF OTHERS**

   Recognize that the authority given to you is not for personal gain or pride, but to serve God and others. Use your authority to bring healing, deliverance, and restoration in the lives of others.

Remember, walking in the authority of Christ is not about personal power or control, but about surrendering to God's will and allowing His power to work through you. By following this strategy, you can experience the transformative power of walking in the authority that Christ has given you.

SCRIPTURES TO STUDY

Matthew 28:18-20 *"And Jesus came and said to them, 'All authority in heaven and on earth has been given to me. Go therefore and make disciples of all nations, baptizing them in the name of the Father and of the Son and of the Holy Spirit, teaching them to observe all that I have commanded you. And behold, I am with you always, to the end of the age.'"*

Luke 10:19 *"Behold, I have given you authority to tread on serpents and scorpions, and over all the power of the enemy, and nothing shall hurt you."*

Colossians 2:9-10 *"For in him the whole fullness of deity dwells bodily, and you have been filled in him, who is the head of all rule and authority."*

2 Timothy 1:7 *"For God gave us a spirit not of fear but of power and love and self-control."*

James 4:7 *"Submit yourselves therefore to God. Resist the devil, and he will flee from you."*

1 John 4:4 *"Little children, you are from God and have overcome them, for he who is in you is greater than he who is in the world."*

These scriptures affirm the authority that Christ has given to His followers and encourage us to walk in that authority with confidence, knowing that we have the power and presence of God with us. They remind us to submit to God, resist the enemy, and rely on the strength and power of Christ.

ASK YOURSELF

- How can I fully understand and embrace the authority that Christ has given me?

_____

_____

_____

_____

- What are some practical ways to exercise my authority in spiritual warfare?

1. _____
2. _____
3. _____
4. _____

STRATEGY 6

ENGAGING IN FASTING AND PRAYER
Matthew 17:21 *"But this kind does not go out except by prayer and fasting."*

Fasting and prayer, when practiced together, offer a powerful combination that brings numerous benefits. Ultimately, the combination of fasting and prayer creates an environment for spiritual growth, increased faith, and a deeper understanding of God's love and purpose for our lives. Here is a strategy to help you effectively engage in fasting and prayer:

1. **SET A CLEAR PURPOSE AND INTENTION**

    Before starting a fast, have a clear purpose in mind. It could be seeking spiritual breakthrough, guidance, healing, or a deeper intimacy with God. Setting a specific intention will help you stay focused and committed throughout the fast.

2. **SEEK GOD'S GUIDANCE**

    Before beginning a fast, spend time in prayer seeking God's guidance and discernment. Ask Him to reveal the type and duration of the fast that would be most beneficial for your spiritual journey.

3. **CHOOSE THE TYPE OF FAST**

    There are different types of fasts, such as a water fast, juice fast, Daniel fast (eating only fruits, vegetables, and grains), or a partial fast (restricting certain foods or meals). Select a type of fast that aligns with your physical health and the guidance you receive from God.

4. **PREPARE PHYSICALLY AND MENTALLY**

   Gradually prepare your body for the fast by reducing the intake of certain foods or caffeine a few days before. Mentally prepare yourself by focusing on the spiritual purpose of the fast and committing to a time of increased prayer and seeking God's presence.

5. **CREATE A PRAYER AND STUDY PLAN**

   Develop a prayer and study plan for the duration of the fast. Set aside specific times for prayer, meditation, and reading the Bible. Consider using a devotional or specific scripture passages to guide your prayer time.

6. **STAY HYDRATED AND TAKE CARE OF YOUR BODY**

   During the fast, drink plenty of water and listen to your body's needs. If you have any health concerns, consult with a medical professional before starting a fast. Remember, fasting is not about punishing the body, but about seeking God's presence and aligning with His will.

7. **ENGAGE IN SPIRITUAL DISCIPLINES**

   Alongside fasting, incorporate other spiritual disciplines such as worship, journaling, silence, and solitude. These practices can help create a conducive environment for hearing from God and deepening your relationship with Him.

8. **SEEK ACCOUNTABILITY AND SUPPORT**

   Consider partnering with a trusted friend or joining a prayer group or community that can provide support and encouragement during your fast. Share your intentions and experiences with them, and pray together.

9. **END THE FAST GRADUALLY**

   As you approach the end of the fast, gradually reintroduce solid foods to your diet. Be mindful of your body's response and continue to seek God's guidance as you transition back to regular eating.

10. **REFLECT AND APPLY INSIGHTS**

    After the fast, take time to reflect on the experience and any insights or revelations you received from God. Consider how you can apply these insights to your daily life and continue to deepen your relationship with Him.

Remember, fasting and prayer are not about earning God's favor or manipulating Him, but about seeking His presence, aligning with His will, and growing in intimacy with Him. By following this strategy, you can engage in fasting and prayer in a meaningful and transformative way.

SCRIPTURES TO STUDY

Matthew 6:16-18: *"And when you fast, do not look gloomy like the hypocrites, for they disfigure their faces that their fasting may be seen by others. Truly, I say to you, they have received their reward. But when you fast, anoint your head and wash your face, that your fasting may not be seen by others but by your Father who is in secret. And your Father who sees in secret will reward you."*

Matthew 17:21 *"But this kind never comes out except by prayer and fasting."*

Joel 2:12 *"Yet even now," declares the Lord, "return to me with all your heart, with fasting, with weeping, and with mourning."*

Ezra 8:23 *"So we fasted and implored our God for this, and he listened to our entreaty."*

Acts 13:2-3 *"While they were worshiping the Lord and fasting, the Holy Spirit said, 'Set apart for me Barnabas and Saul for the work to which I have called them.' Then after fasting and praying, they laid their hands on them and sent them off."*

Isaiah 58:6 *"Is not this the fast that I choose: to loose the bonds of wickedness, to undo the straps of the yoke, to let the oppressed go free, and to break every yoke?"*

Daniel 9:3 *"Then I turned my face to the Lord God, seeking him by prayer and pleas for mercy with fasting and sackcloth and ashes."*

ASK YOURSELF

- How can I incorporate fasting into my spiritual warfare strategy?

　_____
　_____
　_____
　_____

- What are some specific areas or situations in which fasting and prayer can be particularly effective?

1. _____
2. _____
3. _____
4. _____

STRATEGY 7

SPEAKING THE WORD OF GOD

Hebrews 4:12 *"For the word of God is alive and active. Sharper than any double-edged sword, it penetrates even to dividing soul and spirit, joints and marrow; it judges the thoughts and attitudes of the heart."*

The word of God is not just a collection of ancient texts; it is a living and powerful weapon that has the ability to bring down strongholds and overcome any spiritual opposition. When we speak the word of God, we align ourselves with divine truth and tap into the authority and power of God. It serves as a source of encouragement, guidance, and strength, reminding us of God's promises and his faithfulness. Speaking the word of God in warfare not only empowers us, but it also declares our trust and reliance on God's wisdom and sovereignty. It is through the word of God that we can combat negative thoughts, overcome temptations, and stand firm against the enemy's attacks. By speaking the word of God, we invite the Holy Spirit to work in and through us, bringing transformation, breakthroughs, and victory.

Here Is A Strategy To Help You Effectively Speak The Word Of God In Warfare:

1. **KNOW AND STUDY THE WORD**

   Develop a deep understanding of the Bible by studying and meditating on God's Word regularly. Memorize key scriptures that address different areas of spiritual warfare, such as protection, victory, and the defeat of the enemy.

2. **IDENTIFY THE ENEMY'S TACTICS**

   Recognize the strategies and tactics of the enemy in your life. Be aware of areas where you are experiencing spiritual attacks, temptation, or oppression. This awareness will help you choose specific scriptures to counteract those attacks.

3. **DECLARE THE WORD WITH FAITH AND AUTHORITY**

   Speak the Word of God with confidence, knowing that it carries the power to defeat the enemy. Declare scriptures out loud, proclaiming God's promises and truths over your life, situations, and spiritual battles. Speak with authority, knowing that you have been given authority through Christ.

4. **PERSONALIZE AND APPLY THE WORD**

   As you speak the Word, personalize it to your specific circumstances. Replace pronouns with your name or use "I" statements to make the scripture more personal. Apply the scripture to your situation, believing that God's Word is alive and active in your life.

5. **PRAY AND INTERCEDE WITH THE WORD**

   Incorporate the Word of God into your prayers and intercession. Use scriptures as a foundation for your prayers, aligning your requests with God's will and speaking His promises over the situation. Pray with faith, knowing that God's Word is powerful and effective.

6. **MEDITATE ON THE WORD**

    Take time to meditate on the scriptures you are declaring. Reflect on their meaning and allow them to penetrate your heart and mind. Let the truth of God's Word saturate your thoughts and emotions, building up your faith and renewing your mind.

7. **STAND FIRM IN THE WORD**

    When faced with opposition or attacks, stand firm in the truth of God's Word. Resist the lies and schemes of the enemy by speaking and declaring the Word. Use scriptures as your weapon, knowing that they have the power to demolish strongholds and bring victory.

8. **SURROUND YOURSELF WITH THE WORD**

    Immerse yourself in an environment filled with the Word of God. Surround yourself with worship music, podcasts, sermons, and Christian literature that align with the truth of Scripture. This will help reinforce your faith and keep your focus on God's truth.

9. **SEEK ACCOUNTABILITY AND SUPPORT**

    Engage in spiritual community and seek accountability from fellow believers. Share your struggles and victories, and pray together, speaking the Word of God over one another's lives.

This support system will strengthen your faith and provide encouragement in times of spiritual warfare.

10. **WALK IN OBEDIENCE AND LIVE OUT THE WORD**

Let the Word of God guide your actions and decisions. Live a life of obedience to God's commands and teachings, aligning your behavior with the truth of Scripture. As you walk in obedience, you will experience the power of God's Word manifesting in your life.

Remember, speaking the Word of God in warfare is not simply reciting verses, but engaging with the truth and power of God's Word. By following this strategy, you can effectively wield the Word of God as a weapon in spiritual warfare, experiencing victory and breakthrough in your life. Stay rooted in the Word, seek God's guidance, and rely on the Holy Spirit to empower and guide you in speaking the Word with authority.

SCRIPTURES TO STUDY

Ephesians 6:17 *"And take the helmet of salvation, and the sword of the Spirit, which is the word of God."*

Hebrews 4:12 *"For the word of God is living and active, sharper than any two-edged sword, piercing to the division of soul and of spirit, of joints and of marrow, and discerning the thoughts and intentions of the heart."*

Isaiah 55:11 *"So shall my word be that goes out from my mouth; it shall not return to me empty, but it shall accomplish that which I purpose, and shall succeed in the thing for which I sent it."*

2 Corinthians 10:4-5 *"For the weapons of our warfare are not of the flesh but have divine power to destroy strongholds. We destroy arguments and every lofty opinion raised against the knowledge of God, and take every thought captive to obey Christ."*

Psalm 119:11 *"I have stored up your word in my heart, that I might not sin against you."*

Matthew 4:4 *"But he answered, 'It is written, "Man shall not live by bread alone, but by every word that comes from the mouth of God."*

Romans 10:17 *"So faith comes from hearing, and hearing through the word of Christ."*

Psalm 33:6 *"By the word of the Lord the heavens were made, and by the breath of his mouth all their host."*

Proverbs 18:21 *"Death and life are in the power of the tongue, and those who love it will eat its fruits."*

James 1:22 "But be doers of the word, and not hearers only, deceiving yourselves."

ASK YOURSELF

- How can I effectively use the Word of God as a weapon in spiritual warfare?

  _____
  _____
  _____
  _____

- What are some practical ways to speak the Word of God over my life and circumstances?

1. _____
2. _____
3. _____
4. _____

STRATEGY 8

CULTIVATING A LIFESTYLE OF WORSHIP AND PRAISE

Psalm 22:3 *"But you are holy, enthroned in the praises of Israel."*

Having a lifestyle of praise and worship is of utmost importance for several reasons. Firstly, it allows us to cultivate a deep and intimate relationship with the divine. Through praise and worship, we acknowledge the greatness of God and express our gratitude and reverence towards Him. This not only strengthens our connection with the divine, but also brings us peace, joy, and a sense of purpose. Secondly, a lifestyle of praise and worship helps us to shift our focus from ourselves and our circumstances to God. It reminds us that we are not in control, but rather, we surrender to a higher power. This humility and surrender enable us to trust in God's plan and find comfort and guidance in His presence. Lastly, living a lifestyle of praise and worship allows us to be a witness and an example to others. When we consistently express our love for God and live in a state of worship, we inspire and encourage those around us to do the same. Our actions and attitude of praise can bring hope, healing, and transformation to others, inviting them into a relationship with the divine and leading them towards a life of purpose and fulfillment.

True Worship Is Not A Slow Song But It Is A Cry From The Heart.

Strategy For Cultivating A Lifestyle Of Worship And Praise:

1. **START EACH DAY WITH GRATITUDE**

    Begin your day by acknowledging and expressing gratitude for the blessings in your life. This can be done through journaling, prayer, or simply taking a few moments to reflect on what you are grateful for.

2. **SET ASIDE REGULAR TIME FOR PERSONAL WORSHIP**

    Create a daily or weekly routine that includes intentional time for personal worship and praise. This can involve reading sacred texts, meditating, singing hymns or worship songs, or engaging in acts of service.

3. **ATTEND RELIGIOUS SERVICES**

    Make it a priority to regularly attend religious services or gatherings where you can join others in worship and praise. This not only provides an opportunity for communal worship, but also allows you to connect with a supportive community of believers.

4. **PRACTICE MINDFULNESS**

    Cultivate a mindset of mindfulness by being fully present in the moment and intentionally focusing on the divine. This can be done through practices such as deep breathing, meditation, or simply being aware of your thoughts and actions throughout the day.

5. **SURROUND YOURSELF WITH A SUPPORTIVE COMMUNITY**

    Seek out and surround yourself with a community of believers who share your desire to cultivate a lifestyle of worship and praise. This can be done through joining a religious organization, participating in small groups or Bible studies, or connecting with like-minded individuals online.

6. **CONTINUOUSLY SEEK SPIRITUAL GROWTH**

    Commit to a lifelong journey of spiritual growth by regularly reading sacred texts, seeking out opportunities for learning and reflection, and being open to new insights and experiences. This will help deepen your understanding and connection to the divine, and enhance your ability to live a lifestyle of worship and praise.

SCRIPTURES TO STUDY

Psalm 100:4 *"Enter his gates with thanksgiving and his courts with praise; give thanks to him and praise his name."*

Psalm 95:1-2 *"Come, let us sing for joy to the Lord; let us shout aloud to the Rock of our salvation. Let us come before him with thanksgiving and extol him with music and song."*

Colossians 3:16 *"Let the message of Christ dwell among you richly as you teach and admonish one another with all wisdom through psalms, hymns, and songs from the Spirit, singing to God with gratitude in your hearts."*

Hebrews 13:15 *"Through Jesus, therefore, let us continually offer to God a sacrifice of praise—the fruit of lips that openly profess his name."*

Psalm 34:1 *"I will extol the Lord at all times; his praise will always be on my lips."*

Reflecting on these scriptures can help deepen our understanding of worship and praise, and inspire us to live a lifestyle that consistently honors and glorifies God.

ASK YOURSELF

- How can I make worship and praise a regular part of my spiritual warfare strategy?

  _____
  _____
  _____
  _____

- What are some ways to cultivate a heart of worship and praise in all circumstances?

1. _____
2. _____
3. _____
4. _____

STRATEGY 9

SEEKING GODLY COUNSEL AND ACCOUNTABILITY
Proverbs 11:14 *"For lack of guidance a nation falls, but victory is won through many advisers."*

The principle of seeking counsel from a multitude of advisors is crucial for ensuring safety and success on the battlefield. As **Proverbs 24:6** states, *"For by wise guidance you can wage your war, and in abundance of counselors there is victory."* This scripture emphasizes the importance of seeking wise counsel and input from multiple sources, as it leads to effective strategies, informed decision-making, and ultimately, victory in warfare.

Strategy For Seeking Godly Counsel And Accountability:

1. **PRAY FOR GUIDANCE**

    Begin by seeking God's wisdom and direction in finding the right individuals to provide godly counsel and accountability. Ask Him to lead you to trustworthy and spiritually mature people who can support you during this warfare.

2. **CONNECT WITH A LOCAL CHURCH**

    Engage with a local church community where you can find like-minded believers who can offer godly counsel. Attend services, Bible studies, and actively participate in church activities to build relationships with fellow believers.

3. **SEEK OUT SPIRITUAL MENTORS**

   Look for individuals who have a deep understanding of Scripture and a mature walk with God. Approach them and ask if they would be willing to mentor you, providing guidance and accountability in your spiritual journey.

4. **JOIN A DISCIPLESHIP GROUP**

   Many churches or Christian organizations offer discipleship programs where you can receive guidance and accountability from more experienced believers. These groups often provide a structured environment for growth and spiritual development.

5. **ATTEND CONFERENCES OR RETREATS**

   Consider attending conferences or retreats focused on spiritual growth and warfare. These events often provide opportunities to hear from seasoned speakers, interact with other believers, and receive prayer and counsel.

6. **BE OPEN AND HONEST**

   When seeking godly counsel and accountability, it's important to be transparent and vulnerable about your struggles and challenges. This openness allows others to understand your situation better and provide relevant and effective support.

7. **REGULARLY MEET WITH YOUR ACCOUNTABILITY PARTNER**

   Once you have found a godly individual who can serve as your accountability partner, schedule regular meetings to discuss your spiritual journey, challenges, and victories. These meetings can provide a safe space for confession, prayer, and guidance.

8. **STAY GROUNDED IN SCRIPTURE**

   As you seek godly counsel and accountability, always ensure that the advice and guidance you receive align with the teachings of the Bible. Regularly study and meditate on God's Word to discern His will and test the counsel you receive.

Remember, seeking godly counsel and accountability is an ongoing process. Be patient and persistent in your pursuit, and trust that God will provide the right people to support you in the midst of your spiritual warfare.

SCRIPTURES TO STUDY

Proverbs 15:22 *"Without counsel plans fail, but with many advisers they succeed."*

Proverbs 20:18 *"Plans are established by seeking advice; so if you wage war, obtain guidance."*

Proverbs 24:6 *"For by wise guidance you can wage your war, and in abundance of counselors there is victory."*

By incorporating these scriptures into the strategy of seeking counsel and accountability in warfare, we can align our actions with biblical wisdom, ensuring that we make informed decisions and increase our chances of success on the battlefield.

ASK YOURSELF

- How can I surround myself with godly counsel and accountability in spiritual warfare?

  _____

  _____

  _____

- What are some practical ways to seek wise guidance and support from fellow believers?

  1. _____
  2. _____
  3. _____
  4. _____

STRATEGY 10

WALKING IN UNITY WITH THE BODY OF CHRIST

1 Corinthians 12:12 *"Just as a body, though one, has many parts, but all its many parts form one body, so it is with Christ."*

Unity is of utmost importance according to scripture. In **Psalm 133:1,** it says, *"How good and pleasant it is when God's people live together in unity!"* Unity among believers reflects the heart of God and is a powerful testimony to the world. Jesus prayed for unity among his followers in **John 17:21**, saying, *"that all of them may be one, Father, just as you are in me and I am in you."* The apostle Paul also emphasized the importance of unity in **Ephesians 4:3**, urging believers to *"make every effort to keep the unity of the Spirit through the bond of peace."* Unity allows the body of Christ to function as it should, with each member playing their unique role and contributing to the overall health and growth of the church. It is through unity that the body can effectively fulfill its mission of spreading the Gospel and demonstrating God's love to the world.

Strategy for walking in unity with the body of Christ

1. **FOSTER A SPIRIT OF LOVE AND FORGIVENESS**

    In times of warfare, it is crucial to maintain a spirit of love and forgiveness within the body of Christ. The enemy seeks to divide and create discord among believers, but by choosing to love one another and forgive any offenses, we can maintain unity and strength. Remember the words of Jesus in **John 13:35**: *"By this, all people will know that you are my disciples if you have love for one another."*

2. **GUARD AGAINST GOSSIP AND NEGATIVITY**:

   The enemy often uses gossip, negative talk, and divisive attitudes to sow discord within the body of Christ. Be vigilant in guarding your speech and thoughts. Instead, focus on speaking life, encouragement, and edification to others. Choose to build up and support one another, rather than tearing down.

3. **ENGAGE IN SPIRITUAL WARFARE TOGETHER**

   Unity is not just about individual believers walking with Christ; it is also about coming together as a body to engage in spiritual warfare. Join forces with other believers, whether through small groups, prayer meetings, or church gatherings, to intercede for one another and stand against the enemy's attacks. Together, we can be a powerful force for God's kingdom.

4. **STAY FOCUSED ON THE MISSION**

   Remember that our ultimate goal is to advance God's kingdom and share the Gospel. Keep your eyes fixed on Jesus and the mission at hand, allowing His love to guide your actions and decisions.

Walking in love and unity during warfare is not easy, but with God's help and the support of fellow believers, it is possible. Trust in His strength and rely on His Spirit to empower you to love and unite with others, even in the midst of spiritual battles.

SCRIPTURES TO STUDY

Psalm 133:1 *"How good and pleasant it is when God's people live together in unity!"*

John 17:21 *"that all of them may be one, Father, just as you are in me and I am in you. May they also be in us so that the world may believe that you have sent me."*

Ephesians 4:3 *"Make every effort to keep the unity of the Spirit through the bond of peace."*

Romans 12:4-5 *"For just as each of us has one body with many members, and these members do not all have the same function, so in Christ we, though many, form one body, and each member belongs to all the others."*

1 Corinthians 1:10 *"I appeal to you, brothers and sisters, in the name of our Lord Jesus Christ, that all of you agree with one another in what you say and that there be no divisions among you, but that you be perfectly united in mind and thought."*

Colossians 3:14 *"And over all these virtues put on love, which binds them all together in perfect unity."*

Philippians 2:2-3 *"then make my joy complete by being like-minded, having the same love, being one in spirit and of one mind. Do nothing out of selfish ambition or vain conceit. Rather, in humility value others above yourselves."*

ASK YOURSELF

- How can I actively pursue unity with other believers in spiritual warfare?

　　_____
　　_____
　　_____
　　_____

- What are some practical ways to build and maintain unity within the Body of Christ for effective spiritual warfare?

1. _____
2. _____
3. _____
4. _____

CONCLUSION

EMBRACING THE VICTORIOUS LIFE IN SPIRITUAL WARFARE

In this journey through the strategies of war in the spirit realm, we have explored the powerful truths and practical insights that equip us to fight our battles with confidence and faith. We have discovered that our weapons are not carnal, but mighty through God for the pulling down of strongholds. We have learned to put on the whole armor of God, to pray in the Spirit, and to walk in the authority and discernment that Christ has given us. Throughout this guide, we have seen that spiritual warfare is not a passive endeavor but an active pursuit of victory. It requires intentionality, discipline, and a deep reliance on God's power and wisdom. We have learned that victory in spiritual warfare is not just a distant hope but a tangible reality that we can experience in our daily lives.

As we conclude this journey, let us remember that our battles are not fought alone. We have a faithful and mighty God who fights on our behalf. He is our refuge and strength, an ever-present help in times of trouble. With Him as our guide and defender, we can be confident that no weapon formed against us shall prosper.

In our pursuit of victorious living in spiritual warfare, let us continue to cultivate a lifestyle of prayer, worship, and the study of God's Word. Let us remain steadfast in putting on the whole armor of God, discerning the tactics of the enemy, and exercising our spiritual authority. Let us prioritize unity and fellowship with other believers, recognizing the strength that comes from standing together in the battles we face.

As we implement these strategies, we will experience the transformational power of God in our lives. We will witness His deliverance, healing, and restoration. We will see strongholds crumble, chains break, and darkness flee. We will walk in the freedom and victory that Christ has secured for us.

In conclusion, dear reader, may you embrace the victorious life in spiritual warfare. May you stand firm in the truth, equipped with the strategies and weapons that God has provided. May you walk in the confidence of knowing that you are more than a conqueror through Him who loves you. And may you declare with boldness,

"THIS IS HOW I FIGHT MY BATTLES!"

WARFARE PRAYER

Heavenly Father, I come before You in the name of Jesus, acknowledging that You are the Almighty God, the One who fights my battles. I thank You for the wisdom and strategies I have learned from this book, and I ask for Your guidance and empowerment as I conclude this journey.

I declare that I am equipped with the full armor of God: the belt of truth, the breastplate of righteousness, the shoes of the gospel of peace, the shield of faith, the helmet of salvation, and the sword of the Spirit, which is Your Word. I put on this armor now, knowing that it will protect me and enable me to stand firm against the schemes of the enemy.

I declare that I am more than a conqueror through Christ who loves me. I am not a victim, but a victor in every battle I face. I am confident that You go before me, fighting on my behalf. I trust in Your unfailing love and faithfulness.

I pray for discernment and wisdom to recognize the strategies of the enemy. Open my eyes to see beyond the physical realm and understand the spiritual dynamics at play. Help me to discern the enemy's tactics, schemes, and strongholds, and give me the strength and courage to overcome them.

I renounce and reject every lie, deception, and fear that the enemy tries to bring into my life. I declare that my mind is renewed by Your Word, and I have the mind of Christ. I choose to think on things that are true, noble, right, pure, lovely, admirable, excellent, and praiseworthy.

I pray for divine protection over myself, my loved ones, and all those who are connected to me. I plead the blood of Jesus over every area of my life, covering myself and everything that concerns me. I command every plan of the enemy to be exposed and rendered powerless.

I declare victory in every area of my life. I am more than a conqueror through Christ who strengthens me. I will not be discouraged or defeated, for You are with me. I trust in Your promises, knowing that You are faithful to fulfill them.

I renounce and reject any backlash or retaliation from the enemy. I declare that I am covered by the blood of Jesus, and I am hidden in Christ. I take authority over every demonic force that may try to come against me, and I command them to flee in the name of Jesus.

I stand firm in the truth of Your Word, knowing that You are my refuge and strength. I declare that You are my defender and my shield, and I trust in Your unfailing love and faithfulness.

I choose to walk in forgiveness and love, refusing to harbor any bitterness or resentment towards those who may seek to harm me. I release them into Your hands, knowing that vengeance belongs to You. I pray that they would come to know Your love and experience Your grace.

I commit to walking in obedience to Your Word and seeking Your guidance in every situation. I ask for discernment and wisdom to navigate any potential backlash or retaliation. Help me to respond with grace, wisdom, and love, reflecting Your character in all that I do.

Thank You, Lord, for Your protection, provision, and faithfulness. I trust in Your promises and believe that You are fighting on my behalf. I declare that I am more than a conqueror through Christ who strengthens me.

Thank You, Lord, for the strategies, wisdom, and strength You have imparted to me through this book. I commit to walking in obedience to Your Word and seeking Your guidance in every battle I face. May Your name be glorified through my life and may Your kingdom come and Your will be done on earth as it is in heaven.

In Jesus' name, I pray. Amen.

Made in the USA
Columbia, SC
17 September 2023